Original title:
Winter's Edge

Copyright © 2024 Swan Charm
All rights reserved.

Author: Olivia Orav
ISBN HARDBACK: 978-9916-79-945-1
ISBN PAPERBACK: 978-9916-79-946-8
ISBN EBOOK: 978-9916-79-947-5

Pines Shrouded in Mystery

Tall pines whisper low,
Veiled in shadows deep,
Secrets in the breeze,
Where ancient echoes sweep.

Moonlight spills like gold,
Upon their gnarled bark,
Nature's silent watch,
In the stillness, stark.

Footprints lost in time,
A tale yet untold,
Among the tangled roots,
And branches, bold.

Beneath the starry skies,
Whispers float on high,
Stories intertwine,
As the night drifts by.

In the heart of the woods,
Mysteries reside,
The pines hold their breath,
Where the spirits glide.

Snowbound Secrets

A world wrapped in white,
Soft flakes fall like dreams,
Silence blankets all,
In the moon's pale gleams.

Footsteps fade away,
In the frozen night,
Whispers of the past,
In each sparkling sight.

Trees adorned in frost,
Hold secrets untold,
Beneath the frozen crust,
Lies warmth of the old.

Winds carry the tales,
Of lovers long lost,
In the snow's embrace,
Where warmth pays the cost.

As shadows stretch long,
And the cold winds sigh,
Snowbound secrets wait,
Until spring draws nigh.

A Canvas of Ice

Frozen rivers glide,
A tranquil, glassy art,
Nature's masterpiece,
Where silence plays a part.

Tales etched on the frost,
In designs so bold,
Each crack and each line,
A story retold.

Underneath the chill,
Life quietly waits,
In a frozen dream,
Hiding from the fates.

Reflections of stars,
Dance upon the glass,
As night holds its breath,
In a moment's pass.

With every step made,
On this icy sheet,
A canvas of dreams,
Beneath frozen feet.

Frostwoven Stories

In the morning's glow,
Frost weaves its delight,
Stories in the grass,
Glimmer in the light.

Intricate patterns bloom,
Nature's quiet art,
A tapestry of white,
That warms the heart.

Each blade cloaked in ice,
Holds whispers of time,
Frostwoven stories,
In beauty sublime.

As the dawn unfolds,
And the world awakens,
Life stirs underneath,
The frost's gentle shakin'.

With every turn found,
In this winter's grace,
Frostwoven tales shine,
In the sun's embrace.

A Breath of Gelid Air

In the stillness of the night,
Whispers of frost take flight.
Chilled caress on my skin,
Nature's hush, where dreams begin.

Silent shadows dance and sway,
Winds of winter softly play.
Every breath a ghostly sigh,
Underneath the frozen sky.

Crouching under a Flurry

Beneath the swirling, white embrace,
I find shelter, a secret place.
Snowflakes fall, a gentle kiss,
In the chaos, quiet bliss.

Huddled close against the cold,
Stories of winter softly told.
Each flake unique, a fleeting sight,
Yet together, they weave the night.

Frost Flowers on the Windowpane

Intricate patterns, a crystal bloom,
Nature's art, erasing gloom.
A frozen garden, delicate trace,
Life's fleeting touch leaves no space.

Sunrise warms the earth so shy,
But for now, they bid goodbye.
A moment held in gleaming glass,
Time will pass, as all things pass.

Ephemeral Beauty of Snow

Softly drifting from the sky,
Whispers of winter gently sigh.
Each flake holds a secret song,
In their dance, we all belong.

But as the sun begins to rise,
The beauty fades, no sad goodbyes.
In memories, the snow will stay,
Fleeting joy of a winter's day.

Twilight's Frosted Hand

The sun dips low, a blush of gold,
Shadows stretch long, secrets unfold.
Whispers of night in the crisp, cool air,
Nature holds breath, a stillness rare.

Stars emerge, in the velvet sky,
As day turns to night, the world sighs.
A chill wraps close like a tender vow,
As twilight brushes the earth, here and now.

Frosted leaves glimmer, kissed by light,
In the hush of dusk, all feels right.
Moments weave softly, the day's gentle end,
In twilight's grasp, my heart ascends.

The Last Leaf's Goodbye

In the crisp autumn air, a leaf clings tight,
Golden edges shimmer, caught in the light.
With a gentle sigh, it twirls in the breeze,
A dance of farewell among the bare trees.

Whispering stories of seasons long past,
Every moment cherished, and memories cast.
The branches stand stark, a silhouette gray,
As the last leaf whispers, 'I've done my stay.'

Down to the ground, it spirals slow,
A final farewell in the twilight glow.
Covered in silence, it meets the soft earth,
In its quiet departure, we find rebirth.

Dreams in a Crystal Web

In the folds of night, where shadows weave,
A tapestry glimmers, of dreams we believe.
Suspended in time, like stars in the mist,
Each whispering thread, a wish not to resist.

Moonlight dances on the silken strands,
Casting soft glows over slumbering lands.
Entwined in the magic, our spirits take flight,
Chasing the flickers of fading daylight.

Through crystal webs spun with intentions pure,
We navigate realms where our hearts must endure.
Boundless horizons, where the soul might roam,
In the dreams that we cradle, we find our home.

The Stillness of Frozen Time

In the heart of winter, a world stands still,
Snow blankets softly, a serene, white thrill.
Frost paints the branches with delicate care,
As time holds its breath in the crisp, cold air.

Moments suspended, like beads on a thread,
Each flake a whisper of words left unsaid.
In silence we gather, beneath the pale sky,
Finding solace in stillness as seasons drift by.

The clock's ticking halts, in the hush of the night,
A gentle embrace of unending twilight.
In the stillness we seek, to find what is true,
In frozen time's grasp, we renew and pursue.

Soul of the Subzero

Whispers of frost dance in the air,
A silent realm, stripped of despair.
Beneath the blue, shadows take flight,
Hope flickers softly, igniting the night.

Icicles hang like memories bright,
In the cold embrace, the stars ignite.
Glimmers of warmth, a distant echo,
Resilient hearts beneath the snow.

Time drifts slow, like a heavy sigh,
Painting the world as it passes by.
Each crystal flake tells a tale untold,
Of courage found when the nights are cold.

In the quiet, the stillness sings,
Of battles fought and the joy it brings.
For in the depths of the icy sea,
The soul of winter sets us free.

Beneath the weight, the heart will learn,
To dance with shadows, to spark and burn.
In the heart of subzero, life takes its stand,
While frost-kissed dreams weave through the land.

The Last Flame of the Year

As daylight wanes, shadows elongate,
 The flickering fire anticipates.
A warmth that whispers of bygone days,
 In amber glow, our memories blaze.

Leaves of gold wither on the ground,
 In the silence, the echoes resound.
The last flame dances, a brief delight,
 Bathing the world in tender light.

Each spark that rises tells of the past,
Of moments lived that weren't meant to last.
 As winter blankets the earth in gray,
 Our hearts hold fast to this fading ray.

Yet hope ignites in the heart's embrace,
As cherished dreams find their sacred space.
 Farewell to the year, with a soft sigh,
 The last flame flickers as time drifts by.

In the chill of dusk, we hold it near,
The warmth of life, our guiding sphere.
So let us gather, as shadows grow long,
 Together we sing the winter's song.

Ringing Chimes in the Cold

In the frosty air, chimes gently sway,
Echoes of joy in a winter ballet.
They beckon to hearts with a silvery tune,
Awakening dreams beneath the moon.

Frost coats the branches, a crystalline dress,
Nature's whispers, a moment of bliss.
With each soft ring, the spirit takes flight,
Illuminating darkness with pure delight.

Gathered around, we hear the refrain,
The laughter, the love, melting the pain.
In the quiet night, our souls align,
As chimes carry wishes, so pure and divine.

In the chill of the evening, we find our way,
Guided by chimes in the winter's play.
Their melody lingers, a sweet embrace,
Drawing us closer to this sacred space.

So let the wind carry our hopes on high,
Like ringing chimes beneath the sky.
For in every note, a promise unfolds,
With ringing chimes that pierce through the cold.

Beneath the Shimmering Ceiling

Under starlit skies, our dreams take flight,
Beneath the shimmering, mystical sight.
Each star a promise, a story to share,
Woven in whispers that float through the air.

Moonlight glistens on tranquil streams,
Mirroring the fabric of our woven dreams.
In the hush of night, our hearts beat as one,
As shadows dance softly, till the night is done.

Here in the stillness, we find our grace,
A moment of magic in this timeless space.
With every heartbeat, a wish is cast,
Carried on stardust, holding the past.

Beneath the ceiling of shimmering light,
We weave our hopes into the night.
As dawn approaches, we cherish it all,
The dreams and the stars that together we call.

In the quiet hours, our spirits soar,
Beneath the universe, forevermore.
With open hearts, we embrace the night,
Together exploring the boundless light.

Echoes of the Frozen Lake

Whispers chill beneath the stars,
Reflections dance on silver bars.
Footsteps fade in icy breath,
Nature's song of silent death.

Moonlight casts its ghostly glow,
Where shadows linger, secrets flow.
Cracks in ice sing ancient tales,
Of wanderers and winter gales.

Frigid winds weave through the pines,
Casting spells with frosty lines.
Echoes murmur, spirits glide,
On the frozen lake, they bide.

Frosty fingers trace the scene,
An art of white, a tranquil sheen.
Every ripple's brief embrace,
Holds the essence of this place.

Time stands still as night unfolds,
In the stillness, life beholds.
With every breath, a story wakes,
In echoes of the frozen lakes.

Barefoot on Ice

Barefoot on the shards so clear,
Gliding forth without a fear.
The world around is hushed and white,
Beneath the frosty, starry night.

With every step, my spirit flies,
Kissed by frost and chilly skies.
Waltzing gracefully on a gleam,
Awake and lost within a dream.

The frozen surface, smooth as glass,
Reflecting moments as they pass.
Each movement comes with subtle grace,
A dance of joy in this still space.

Laughter echoes, cuts the cold,
Memories of warmth retold.
In solitude, I find my spark,
As stars ignite the frozen dark.

Barefoot on the ice, I roam,
In this realm, I feel at home.
Nature's whispers fill the air,
A symphony beyond compare.

Crystal Shards of Twilight

Twilight cloaks the world in blue,
As daylight bids the night adieu.
Crystal shards begin to gleam,
Encasing moments in a dream.

Frosted branches gently sway,
In this serene, enchanted way.
Each glimmer tells a tale untold,
Of fleeting warmth and winter's cold.

The horizon melts in hues of pink,
And silver lines begin to link.
In quiet whispers, shadows fall,
Embracing softly, nature's call.

Every breath, a pearl of mist,
In twilight's arms, we can't resist.
The world transformed, a mystic sight,
In the magic of the night.

With open hearts, we stand amazed,
In crystal shards, our souls are grazed.
As twilight weaves its spell so bright,
Our dreams take flight, in muted light.

Hibernation Lullabies

Softly now, the world will sleep,
In blankets thick, the silence deep.
Hibernation's gentle call,
Cradles life, both large and small.

Whispers wrap the trees in peace,
As nature's song begins to cease.
A lullaby, sweet and low,
Guiding creatures through the snow.

Underneath the icy crust,
Dreamers drift in warmth and trust.
The earth holds tight, a slumbering shell,
In the hush, all is well.

Frozen rivers, silent streams,
Reflecting soft and silver beams.
Beneath the frost, the heartbeat slows,
In this haven, tranquility grows.

Lullabies of winter's grace,
Each heartbeat finds its resting place.
In hibernation's sweet embrace,
The world awaits the spring's embrace.

Stars over Hoarfrost

In the still of night, they gleam,
Whispers from the sky's dark seam.
Frozen ground beneath my feet,
Silent world, tranquil and sweet.

Winds caress the icy field,
Nature's beauty softly revealed.
Stars like diamonds up so high,
Painting dreams across the sky.

Every twinkle tells a tale,
Of winter's magic, cold and pale.
Hoarfrost dances in the light,
Wrapping shadows, holding tight.

Underneath the cosmic glow,
Quiet wonders softly flow.
In this moment, time stands still,
Hearts anew, with hope to fill.

Beneath stars, the night so clear,
Embracing deep, the soul draws near.
Awash in silver, night's embrace,
In the hoarfrost, find my place.

Glacial Serenade

Crystalline whispers fill the air,
Echoes of beauty, cold yet rare.
Mountains rise in glimmering glow,
A serenade of ice and snow.

Softly drifting, flakes descend,
Nature's song, the perfect blend.
Glaciers move with timeless grace,
Carving deep their ancient trace.

Underneath the azure skies,
Nature hums, a lullaby.
Icebergs float in tranquil seas,
Gentle sways in winter's breeze.

A symphony of frost and light,
Guiding stars through endless night.
Each note sings of dreams anew,
Wrapped in white, the world feels true.

As echoes fade and silence reigns,
The glacial song softly remains.
In every breath, the beauty felt,
In frozen tears, my heart is dealt.

Bare Branches and Shimmering Clouds

Bare branches stretch towards the sky,
Silent witnesses as time goes by.
Shimmering clouds in twilight's dance,
Nature's canvas, a fleeting glance.

Soft whispers in the cool night air,
Dreams of spring, a distant care.
Each branch holds stories yet untold,
Of summer's warmth and winter's cold.

Golden hues as daylight fades,
Reflecting on the forest glades.
Clouds like cotton, soft and white,
A perfect backdrop for the night.

In the stillness, shadows play,
Echoes of the light decay.
As dusk wraps around the trees,
Nature breathes in gentle pleas.

The merging of the dark and light,
Promises hope with morning bright.
Bare branches sway, their story bold,
While shimmering clouds their secrets hold.

Threads of Silver in the Gloom

In the silence where shadows lie,
Threads of silver weave and sigh.
Whispers of the night unfold,
Mysteries of the dark retold.

Moonlight spills on ancient trees,
Dancing softly in the breeze.
Glimmers shine through velvet air,
Each moment wrapped in whispered care.

Darkness cradles tender dreams,
Lit by stars with soft, bright beams.
Threads of silver softly gleam,
Weaving life into the dream.

In the gloom, a flicker bright,
A beacon calls to hearts in flight.
Through the shadows, hope reveals,
The warmth that tender darkness heals.

Let the night and silver thread,
Guide the paths that lie ahead.
In the tapestry of the night,
Threads of silver bring the light.

Song of the Lonely Hearth

In the stillness of the night,
A fire flickers, soft and bright.
Shadows dance upon the wall,
In this solitude, I feel so small.

Embers crackle, tales untold,
Whispers of warmth, the night grows cold.
Each spark a memory, deeply sown,
In this lonely hearth, I find my own.

A gentle sigh, the flames take flight,
Embrace the quiet, hold on tight.
The glow reveals the path ahead,
In this stillness, dreams are fed.

Outside the world may rush and spin,
But here, it's peace I find within.
Lonely hearth, my faithful friend,
In your warmth, my heart can mend.

So let the storm rage wild and fierce,
Inside, my spirit you will pierce.
With every flicker, I hold fast,
To the lonely song that will ever last.

Shivers of an Unseen Wind

Whispers wrap the twilight air,
Brittle leaves dance, free from care.
A shiver runs through branches bare,
The unseen wind begins to share.

Softly haunting, it calls my name,
Through the night, a ghostly flame.
In shadows deep, it spins its tale,
An echoing song, a gentle wail.

Cold breath stirs the silent ground,
In every rustle, secrets found.
The world sleeps on with weary sighs,
While beneath the stars, the shivers rise.

Moonlit paths where shadows creep,
Guarded dreams start to leap.
In the chill, my spirit finds,
The unseen wind that binds our minds.

With every gust, my heart takes flight,
Into the depths of the mysterious night.
For in the shivers, I am free,
Lost in the dance of eternity.

Twilight's Respite

As day gives way to dusk's embrace,
A tender hush fills every space.
The sky, awash in shades of gold,
Whispers stories long since told.

Stars awaken, one by one,
Night's symphony has just begun.
The moon hangs low, a watchful eye,
In twilight's arms, the world draws nigh.

Gentle breezes weave through trees,
Capturing scents carried with ease.
In this moment, time stands still,
Heartbeats soft beneath the chill.

A tranquil peace descends like dew,
In the fading light, all feels new.
Thoughts wander like the fireflies,
Chasing dreams beneath dark skies.

Twilight holds its breath for me,
In the quiet, I'm truly free.
A sanctuary where shadows weave,
In this respite, I gently leave.

Echoes of an Old Hearth

Flickering flames tell tales of yore,
In this space, I find the core.
Memories dance in shadows cast,
Echoes of laughter from the past.

The walls hold whispers, soft and low,
An unbroken thread in time's flow.
Faded voices, warm and near,
In the old hearth, I shed a tear.

Seasons change, yet here I stay,
Wrapped in warmth that won't decay.
Beneath the watchful, flickering light,
Ghostly stories come to life at night.

Crackling wood, a soothing song,
In this embrace, I feel I belong.
The heart of home, steadfast and true,
Echoes of love come shining through.

So let the flames ignite my dreams,
With every spark, a world redeems.
In the hearth's glow, I find my place,
In echoes of time, I meet my grace.

The Thaw of Remembrance

Beneath the ice, memories lie,
Soft whispers of days gone by.
With each warm ray, they start to melt,
The heart's old wounds begin to felt.

In the gentle light, they shimmer bright,
Echoes of laughter, pure delight.
The past unfurls like blooming flowers,
Awakening hope in springtime hours.

Every droplet carries a dream,
Reflections dancing in a stream.
As the world in colors reclaims,
Lost names rise up like old, sweet flames.

Crisp air carries unspoken songs,
Tales of where the heart belongs.
With each breath, the sorrow fades,
In the sun's warmth, love cascades.

As the frost gives way to green,
New chapters form where once had been.
A lively spirit starts to grow,
In the golden light of the thawed glow.

Cedar's Cloak of Ice

Under heavy snow, the cedars stand,
Draped in white by winter's hand.
Silent sentinels of the night,
Guarding secrets, pure and bright.

Branches bending low with grace,
Carrying winter's cold embrace.
Each limb adorned with crystal lace,
Nature's art, a frozen space.

When the sun shines, they catch the light,
Flickering diamonds, a stunning sight.
In the quiet, a world of peace,
Cedar's cloak, a sweet release.

Birds find refuge in their boughs,
While the wind whispers timeless vows.
Nature cradles life so gently,
In the cold, it thrives intently.

As seasons shift, the ice will break,
Revealing wonders, a new path to take.
The cedars will stand, steadfast and true,
With stories of winters, old and new.

Evening's Frostbitten Kiss

The sun descends with a tender sigh,
Painting the sky, where shadows lie.
Cool whispers brush upon the land,
Evening's chill, a lover's hand.

Each step sparks a breath of smoke,
A winter's spell, a soft cloak.
Stars awaken as daylight wanes,
In the silence, beauty reigns.

Frostbite kisses linger sweet,
Nipping gently at tired feet.
The night unfolds its silver quilt,
Wrapping the earth, calm and wilt.

In the glow of the moon's embrace,
Time slows down, a sacred space.
Every moment, a fleeting bliss,
Captured in evening's frosty kiss.

Whispers of dreams drift through the air,
Laden with hope, a gentle prayer.
As the stars twinkle, memories gleam,
In the deep night, we chase the dream.

The Ghost of Summer Past

In the golden light, shadows play,
Echoes of laughter, bright and gay.
Whispers of warmth in every breeze,
Memories stir among the trees.

A fading sun, soft hues abound,
Crisp leaves tumble to the ground.
The ghost of summer, lingering,
In every note the crickets sing.

Gardens housed in vibrant dreams,
Now softly drift like whispered themes.
The scent of blossoms, sweet and rare,
Reminds us of a season's flare.

In every shadow, stories weave,
Of sun-soaked days and hearts that believe.
Though winter's chill has come to stay,
The warmth of summer lights our way.

As frost covers the earth like lace,
We cherish sunshine's warm embrace.
In our hearts, summer never goes,
A timeless dance, where memory flows.

The Veil of Frosted Mornings

A silver veil on grassy ground,
The world wrapped in a hushed sound.
Each breath a whisper, crisp and clear,
Morning's magic drawing near.

Frosty crystals cling to dreams,
Nature's canvas, bright it gleams.
Birds sing soft, their voices low,
In the light, the colors glow.

The sun peeks through, a gentle strain,
Warmth returns to melt the pain.
Promises of spring's embrace,
Hidden under winter's grace.

Footsteps crunch on pristine white,
Children's laughter, pure delight.
Every moment, frozen time,
Nature's rhythm, a silent rhyme.

In this haven, still and bright,
Morning dances with delight.
A moment brief, but heart will keep,
The magic found in moments deep.

When Silence Falls

When silence falls, the world stands still,
The echo of a distant thrill.
Stars emerge from evening's cloak,
While shadows whisper, softly spoke.

Night enfolds the weary day,
In twilight's arms, we drift away.
The moon hangs low, a silver thread,
Guiding thoughts where dreamers tread.

In every hush, the heart will hear,
All the whispers, far and near.
Magic swirls in the gentle breeze,
A promise hangs among the trees.

When silence falls, the mind takes flight,
Into realms of dark and light.
Time slips by, a fleeting grace,
In this quiet, we find our place.

The stars align, a cosmic call,
In the stillness, we find our all.
When silence wraps the world in peace,
Sweet moments linger, never cease.

Evening's Chill

The sun dips low, a gentle sigh,
As day gives way to night's deep sky.
Cool breezes dance through fading light,
Evening's chill embraces night.

Colors fade to shades of gray,
The warmth of day slips far away.
Whispers creep as shadows grow,
In the stillness, soft and slow.

A blanket wraps the sleeping earth,
In the calm, we find our worth.
Stars ignite in velvet space,
Nighttime holds a quiet grace.

Coolness settles, edges blur,
The heart beats soft, a gentle purr.
In evening's grip, we find our rest,
Wrapped in dreams, we are our best.

The world at peace, so calm, so still,
In evening's chill, with time to fill.
Moments stretch like shadows long,
In twilight's arms, we all belong.

Lament of the Frosted Pines

Amidst the woods where silence reigns,
The frosted pines hold hidden pains.
Each branch a story, aching, bold,
A tapestry of whispers told.

Beneath the weight of winter's breath,
They stand in quiet, mocking death.
Yet still they reach for light above,
In every bough, a hint of love.

When snowflakes dance on gentle air,
The pines stand strong against despair.
A muted cry, a frosty song,
In nature's arms, we all belong.

The forest sleeps, yet dreams awake,
In every step, the earth will shake.
Frosted limbs will warm with time,
In spring's embrace, a past sublime.

Lamenting tales the pines will share,
Of battles fought and evening air.
Through seasons' turn, they stand and sway,
In silence found, their hearts will stay.

Clouds of Glistening White

Clouds drift softly in the blue,
A canvas painted, bright and new.
Glistening white, they float on by,
Whispers of dreams in the vast sky.

They cradle secrets, light as air,
Dancing gently without a care.
The sun peeks through with a golden ray,
Brightening hearts throughout the day.

Above, they gather, a fleeting show,
In shapes and patterns, ebb and flow.
Children laugh and point to the skies,
Finding wonders with wide-eyed eyes.

But as the hours begin to wane,
The clouds can shift with sudden rain.
A reminder of change that comes so fast,
Still, beauty lingers, forever to last.

The Color of Cold

Beneath the frost, the earth does sleep,
A blanket soft, embracing deep.
Whispers of winter touch the ground,
In hues of blue, the silence found.

The breath of air, a crystal mist,
Each moment fleeting, but hard to resist.
Branches glisten, a sparkling lace,
Nature's artwork, a frozen grace.

Shadows stretch as daylight fades,
A quiet peace, where stillness wades.
The sky, a canvas of twilight gray,
Holds the promise of another day.

Wrapped in layers, warm and snug,
We watch the world, a gentle hug.
In the color of cold, we find delight,
A comfort wrapped in the sheer frost light.

A Quietude of Snow

Snowflakes fall like whispered sighs,
Blanketing earth beneath soft skies.
In the hush, a stillness profound,
A quietude where peace is found.

Trees wear white like crowns of cheer,
As every sound seems crystal clear.
Footprints mark the path we tread,
In this soft world where dreams are spread.

Children playing in purest glee,
Building castles hand in hand, carefree.
Laughter echoes in the cold,
Stories of warmth in the winter's fold.

As night descends, the stars ignite,
Reflecting on the snow so bright.
Each twinkling light a gentle glow,
In the magic of a quietude of snow.

Rediscovering Silence

In the stillness, we find our way,
Amid the chaos of everyday.
A moment captured, time stands still,
Whispers of peace, a soothing thrill.

Voices fade, as shadows creep,
Into the heart where secrets sleep.
Rediscovering silence, layers deep,
A sacred space for thoughts to leap.

The world retreats, a soft embrace,
In quietude, we find our place.
Breathe in slowly, let calm prevail,
Listen closely, hear the tale.

Nature hums a gentle tune,
Beneath the sun, beneath the moon.
In the silence, we come alive,
In every heartbeat, dreams revive.

Sweet Surrender to the Chill

Soft whispers of the frost,
Kissing cheeks with tender grace,
Nights wrapped in a silken coat,
Stars twinkle in their cold embrace.

The world shivers in delight,
Blankets woven from pure snow,
Dreams dance in the silver light,
As the chill begins to grow.

Breathe in deep the winter air,
Fresh and crisp like morning dew,
Nature sings a loving prayer,
In this season of the blue.

Trees stand tall, their branches bare,
Crystals spark the dusk's descent,
Underneath the moon's soft glare,
We find peace in quiet content.

As we twirl in frosty glee,
My heart warms to winter's song,
In this sweet serenity,
Where the chill feels like belonging.

Solstice Shadows

Longer nights with whispers low,
Flickering flames in a cozy room,
Echoes of the season's flow,
Drift into a gentle gloom.

Figures dance in shifting light,
Shadows stretch across the floor,
Every flicker, a delight,
Stories woven, forever more.

The world slows in twilight's hue,
Wrapped in warmth, both near and far,
Every moment feels so true,
Underneath the evening star.

Breath of winter fills the air,
Promise of the year to come,
In the silence, there's a prayer,
For new journeys, hope, and drum.

Together, we embrace the night,
Every shadow a friend divine,
In the soft, enchanting light,
Solstice whispers, hearts align.

Treading Lightly in White

Footprints trace a whispered path,
In the quiet, snowflakes fall,
Nature's beauty stirs a laugh,
As we wander, heed the call.

Gentle flakes on upturned face,
Laughter mingles with the breeze,
In this bright and wondrous space,
Time stands still beneath the trees.

Each step soft, a careful dance,
Crystals glimmer, spark and shine,
Winter's beauty holds a chance,
To embrace the pure divine.

Captured in a frosty dream,
Magic lingers on the air,
Every moment feels like cream,
Rich and soft, beyond compare.

Hand in hand, we take the trail,
Leaning into winter's sway,
In this white world, love won't fail,
Treading lightly, come what may.

Clusters of Crystal

Tiny jewels on branches cling,
Draped in diamond, purest light,
Nature whispers, softly sing,
Clusters of crystal, calm delight.

Each glimmer tells a story sweet,
Boundless beauty in the air,
Where earth and sky in silence meet,
Moments freeze with gentle care.

Fingers reach to touch the frost,
Every breath a shimmering song,
In this world where time feels lost,
Together, we are bold and strong.

Beneath the sun, the sparkles play,
Magic spun from winter's loom,
Casting all my cares away,
In the warmth of nature's bloom.

With every step, a mindful grace,
In the clusters of crystal's hold,
Winter's wonder finds its place,
In a story yet untold.

Requiem for a Fading Leaf

Once vibrant green, now turning brown,
A whispering breeze, no longer proud.
In the dance of time, a gentle bow,
A fleeting moment, lost in the crowd.

Crimson edges, the twilight's song,
Each fluttering fall, a soft goodbye.
Nature's sorrow, where do we belong?
Beneath the trees, where memories lie.

To the ground, a soft embrace,
Life's cycle spins, the earth will mourn.
In every curve, a story traced,
Of seasons lost, and dreams reborn.

Gone are the days of sunlit grace,
Where laughter danced, in shadows cast.
With every gust, the winds erase,
The vibrant hues that couldn't last.

In quiet corners, the stillness grows,
A requiem sung for what once was.
In the silence, the heart well knows,
All beauty fades, as gently does.

Creep of the Cold

The shadows stretch as daylight fades,
A chilling touch begins to creep.
The breath of winter, unseen shades,
Invades the air, enticing sleep.

Moonlit nights grow long and bare,
The frost adorns each windowpane.
Trees bow low in the frigid air,
While whispers hum a lonesome strain.

Footsteps crunch on frosty ground,
Sound diminished, echoes hushed.
In this silence, peace is found,
While the world outside is slowly crushed.

Waves of twilight, a gray attire,
Embrace the earth in icy hands.
With every breath, a spark of fire,
Burns in the hearts of winter's bands.

Through the stillness, winter glows,
A quiet magic spun from night.
As stars emerge, a secret flows,
In the creep of cold, a soft delight.

Frost-Kissed Horizons

At dawn, the light, a gentle brush,
Paints the sky in soft embrace.
With every hue, the world will hush,
As frosted fields take on their grace.

Silver whispers kiss the ground,
A delicate touch on blades of grass.
In silence, beauty can be found,
As moments pause, and hours pass.

The rising sun, a golden flame,
Ignites the frost with warming glow.
Each sparkle dances, none the same,
Inviting hearts to bask and flow.

Nature's canvas, pure and bright,
Draws the eye to distant dreams.
As day unfolds, it feels just right,
In quiet realms, where hope redeems.

Frost-kissed horizons, vast and wide,
A promise held in morning's grace.
With every step, we walk beside,
The magic found in nature's face.

Chilling Whispers of Dawn

In the hush of dawn's first light,
Chilling whispers brush the trees.
Shadows linger, fading night,
As nature stirs in timeless ease.

Softly breaking, the day awakes,
With every breath, the world feels new.
In whispered tones, the silence shakes,
A symphony of morning dew.

Misty veils upon the lake,
A landscape mirrored, cold and clear.
Each ripple tells, a secret wake,
In tranquil notes, for all to hear.

The sun ascends, yet chills remain,
With every heartbeat, life unfolds.
In every breath, a hint of pain,
And fragile warmth as nature scolds.

Chilling whispers, sweet and soft,
Draw us close to the day anew.
In every beat, our spirits loft,
As dawn breaks forth in vibrant view.

Shimmering Veils of Cold

Veils of frost glisten bright,
Under the pale moonlight.
Whispers dance upon the air,
A chill that tingles with flair.

Frozen breath paints the night,
Stars twinkle, such delight.
Nature dons a crystal crown,
In this slumber, we won't drown.

Each flake a fleeting art,
Nature's beauty, set apart.
A world wrapped in icy grace,
Where time slows its frantic pace.

Through the silence, secrets weave,
In this wonder, we believe.
With each step, a story unfolds,
In shimmering veils of cold.

Beneath the frosty glow,
Mysterious shadows flow.
The night sways, a gentle sigh,
As dreams and winter intertwine.

Forgotten Footsteps in Snow

Amidst the white, a trail lost,
Each footprint tells of the cost.
A journey taken, now concealed,
In winter's grasp, all revealed.

Echoes linger in the freeze,
Whispered tales in the trees.
Silent stories left behind,
In the snow, memories bind.

Frosted paths where shadows tread,
Ghostly figures roam, now fled.
Forgotten dreams blanket the ground,
In this stillness, lost is found.

Time flows like a gentle stream,
In the cold, we chase a dream.
Yet the footprints fade away,
As dawn breaks on a brand new day.

In the hush, a heart can yearn,
For the lessons we learn.
Forgotten steps in the snow,
Mark the paths of hearts aglow.

The Painter's Palette of Ice

A canvas of frost, vast and wide,
Where colors of winter coincide.
Blues and whites, a tranquil blend,
Nature's artistry shall not end.

Brushstrokes of shimmers unfold,
Every hue a story told.
Icicles hang in perfect form,
In this palette, beauty's warm.

Crystalline shards catch the light,
Dancing prisms, pure delight.
With each gust, colors change,
Winter's vision, ever strange.

The artist's hand, unseen yet clear,
Crafts a world, so sincere.
In the silence, creation sings,
From the cold, inspiration springs.

Amidst the chill, a vibrant tone,
In every frost, a beauty grown.
The painter's palette spans the skies,
In the winter's grasp, magic lies.

Glacial Silence

In the stillness, the world holds breath,
Wrapped in layers, the hush of death.
Glaciers breathe a quiet sigh,
Under the weight of the blue sky.

Endless stretches of unmarked white,
Where echoes shatter into silence bright.
A moment frozen, time stands still,
In this realm, nature finds its will.

The vastness hums a gentle tune,
Under the watch of the silver moon.
Whispers of the ancient freeze,
Carried softly on the breeze.

Amidst the frost, a serene grace,
In this quiet, we find our place.
Each crystal spark, a breathless glance,
In glacial silence, we find our chance.

To listen to the whispers low,
Of tales in the ice and snow.
In every still, a wonder grows,
In the heart of glacial repose.

Embraced by the Shroud

In the night, shadows creep,
Whispers in the air so deep.
Wrapped in a veil, soft and tight,
Dreams are born in the stillness of night.

Veils of mist dance on the ground,
Nature's silence, a sacred sound.
Each breath lingers, calm and slow,
While the world fades, wrapped in glow.

Stars peer through, a gentle light,
Guiding souls lost in the night.
Embraced by shadows, we find our way,
In the warmth of night, we long to stay.

Hands together, hearts in prayer,
Finding solace in the air.
In this moment, time stands still,
As we yield to the night's sweet thrill.

Embraced by dreams, we softly sway,
In the shroud where we wish to stay.
Each heartbeat echoes in the dark,
A dance of souls, a living spark.

Frosted Fables

Days of wonder wrapped in white,
Stories told by the pale moonlight.
Frosted branches, glistening bright,
Whispering secrets of the night.

Children laugh, and snowflakes play,
Creating magic in their sway.
Every footprint, a tale to tell,
In the silence where lost dreams dwell.

Icicles hang like crystal chains,
Capturing sunlight, breaking pains.
Nature's canvas, an artist's dream,
Where frost and fire twine and scheme.

Among the trees, shadows prance,
In the chill, we take a chance.
Underneath the cosmic glow,
Frosted fables come and go.

As night descends, the world feels small,
In the frost, we hear the call.
A whisper of warmth in the winter's bite,
Frosted fables basking in light.

The Calm Before the Melt

Quiet whispers fill the space,
Nature holds its breath, a grace.
Snowflakes gather, soft and deep,
In this moment, silence we keep.

Heavy clouds, a brooding sky,
Waiting for the sun to rise high.
Each glimmer, a promise anew,
In the stillness, dreams break through.

Time pauses, a world in dreams,
Echoes of laughter, soft moonbeams.
Gathered warmth in the crisp cold air,
Preparing hearts for the seasons rare.

Tender moments, fleeting glows,
Nature's dance, the cycle flows.
A breath held tight, the earth in slumber,
The calm before the storms of thunder.

Embrace the hush, the soft caress,
For soon will come nature's undress.
In every thaw, beauty unveils,
The calm before the melt prevails.

Threads of Silence in Silver Light

Underneath the silver moon,
Threads of silence softly croon.
In the night, dreams start to weave,
Secrets held as we believe.

Gentle whispers brush the ground,
In the stillness, life is found.
Every sparkle tells a tale,
In the night, where shadows sail.

Woven moments, a tapestry,
In the dark, we long to be.
Threads of fate, in silver light,
Binding hearts in the quiet night.

Softly drifting, time unfolds,
Within the silence, truth beholds.
A world adorned in shimmering grace,
Threads of silence, our warm embrace.

In the glow, a promise stays,
Wrapped in stillness, love conveys.
Together we dance, souls take flight,
Threads of silence in silver light.

Whispering Pines in the Storm

Whispers rise in the pines,
As the tempest roars above.
Branches sway, gently entwined,
Nature's voice, a tender love.

Raindrops dance on thickened bark,
Echoes of thunder roll near.
Amidst the night, a soft spark,
Guides lost spirits, calms their fear.

Shadows flicker, bright and fleet,
Winds carry secrets untold.
Footsteps falter, hearts still beat,
In the storm, the brave are bold.

Through the chaos, strength is found,
Roots hold fast to the ground wide.
Pine trees whisper all around,
A timeless grace where they bide.

When the storm clouds start to fade,
Silence blankets the weary night.
In the aftermath, hope displayed,
Whispering pines fill hearts with light.

Reflections in a Crystal Pool

Beneath the trees, a still embrace,
A pool reflects the sky's blue grace.
Gentle ripples dance with the breeze,
Whispers of secrets lost in the leaves.

Clouds mirror soft in tranquil depths,
Nature's canvas, a world adept.
Fish glide quietly, shadows play,
Serene moments, drifting away.

Sunbeams filter through branches high,
Painting patterns as they sigh.
Each flicker of light, a fleeting call,
Echoes of beauty, enchanting all.

Time unravels in quiet bliss,
Here, every glance feels like a kiss.
The essence of peace in each glance found,
Reflecting hearts, connecting the ground.

As dusk descends, colors blend,
A borrowed beauty that won't end.
In the crystal pool's soft glow,
Questions linger, answers flow.

The Warmth of a World Turned Cold

In winter's grip, shadows fall,
Nature holds her breath, silent call.
Frosty breaths on windowpanes,
Whispers of warmth in icy veins.

Ash blankets the sun, forlorn,
Yet hearts glow bright, love reborn.
Through every storm, through endless night,
Hope twinkles softly, a guiding light.

Footsteps crunch on a snowy lane,
Memories held in each tiny grain.
Together we stand, hand in hand,
Finding warmth in a frozen land.

Fireplaces crackle, stories weave,
In cold we find what we believe.
Embers glowing, flickers of faith,
Binding our souls in winter's wraith.

So though the world may feel so stark,
In our hearts, love leaves a mark.
Warmth ignites in the coldest time,
Resilient spirits, forever climb.

Puppets of Light in the Gloom

In the shadows, figures sway,
Dancing whispers in dismay.
Threads of silver, stitched with care,
Puppets of light in darkened air.

Glow of lanterns flickers bright,
Carving paths through the endless night.
With every pull, the shadows creep,
A silent promise, dreams to keep.

Hearts beat softly, laughter swells,
Echoing through the hidden dells.
Though gloom surrounds, we rise and play,
With strands of hope that guide the way.

Fingers dance in the twilight's fold,
Stories of courage, of love retold.
Each puppet a tale, vibrant and true,
In the gloom, a world anew.

So let us tread with patient grace,
In the dark, we find our place.
Puppets of light, hand in hand,
Together we spark, together we stand.

Breath of the Frost Moon

In the stillness of the night,
The frost moon glows so bright.
Whispers dance upon the breeze,
Nature sighs and finds its ease.

Branches bare, adorned with ice,
A tranquil realm, so cold, so nice.
Stars above in silence stare,
In this beauty, none compare.

Shadows stretch across the ground,
In this moment, peace is found.
Crystals shimmer, soft and clear,
Frosted air, the heart draws near.

Time slows down, the world at rest,
Underneath the moon's behest.
Gentle tides of winter's breath,
In the chill, we find our depth.

Nature whispers, soft and low,
Where the frosted rivers flow.
A tranquil night, all is well,
In the frost moon's magic spell.

Glimmers of Crystal Twilight

As twilight falls, the shadows creep,
In crystal forms, the night will sweep.
Glimmers dance on every tree,
A sparkling world, wild and free.

Colors blend, a painter's touch,
Moments linger, oh, so much.
Silhouettes of dreams take flight,
In the glow of fading light.

Time suspends in soft embrace,
As day gives way to night's grace.
Underneath the starry veil,
Silent whispers start to trail.

Breezes sigh with secrets old,
Stories of the night unfold.
In this realm of twilight's hue,
Every moment feels brand new.

Glimmers spark in every glance,
Nature's beauty, a sweet dance.
As crystals twinkle, hearts will sway,
In twilight's charm, we wish to stay.

The Quieting of Nature

When the world begins to slow,
In the hush, our hearts will grow.
Softly falls the evening shade,
In this peace, we are remade.

Leaves drop softly to the ground,
In silence, solace can be found.
The rustling whispers start to fade,
A calming balm, the night parade.

Stars peek through the veil of night,
Each one twinkles, pure delight.
Nature's rhythms, depth of sound,
In this quiet, life unbound.

Dusk envelops, softly, sweet,
An embrace where shadows meet.
In the shadows, wander dreams,
Amidst the stillness, hope redeems.

Nature's heart beats ever slow,
In the quiet, love will grow.
Finding peace in muted hues,
In the stillness, we renew.

Frost-Laden Dreams

In the morn, a crystal sheen,
Frosted fields, a winter scene.
Dreams unfold in silver light,
Whispers carried through the night.

Every blade dressed in white lace,
Nature dons her frozen grace.
Breezes blow with gentle cheer,
Echoes soft, the world draws near.

Colors muted, bright as stars,
Frost-kissed landscapes, near and far.
In this beauty, moments gleam,
Awakening our deepest dream.

Silhouettes against the dawn,
Frost-laden dreams gently yawn.
As sunlight kisses icy trees,
Magic stirs on winter's breeze.

In the still, we find our way,
Chasing dreams of yesterday.
Through the frost, our spirits soar,
In this dreamland, we explore.

Fractured Sunlight

Through leaves it breaks, a golden dance,
Shadows shift, as if in trance.
Each beam a story, softly told,
Warmth against the autumn cold.

In fleeting moments, time stands still,
Nature whispers, hearts to fill.
A canvas painted, bold and bright,
Awakens dreams in fractured light.

The world adorned in softest hues,
A treasure found in morning dew.
Glimmers of hope in twilight's fall,
Fractured sunlight, binding all.

Glistening paths, where shadows creep,
Promises made, and secrets keep.
Each ray ignites the silent air,
Fractured sunlight, beyond compare.

A fleeting glance, a moment's grace,
In nature's arms, we find our place.
Lost in echoes, gentle and bright,
Embraced by warmth, in fractured light.

Barren Branches Against the Sky

In winter's grip, the branches bare,
Reach like fingers through cold air.
A silent plea, a whispered sigh,
Barren branches against the sky.

Where once was life, now shadows dwell,
Each gnarled limb a tale to tell.
Of seasons passed, of blooms that flew,
In barren silence, hope renews.

Skyward stretching, yearning still,
For warmer winds, for springtime's thrill.
The chill of night, the breath of day,
Barren branches, poised to sway.

In twilight's glow, they stand so grand,
Guardians of a frozen land.
Against the dusk, they hold their rise,
Barren branches against the sky.

Yet in the void there beats a heart,
Awaiting spring, a brand new start.
Through cold and dark, they silently try,
To dance once more, against the sky.

A Tapestry of White

In winter's hush, the world awakes,
A canvas pure, where silence breaks.
Each flake that falls, a story spun,
A tapestry of white begun.

Blanketing earth in cotton dreams,
Where laughter echoes, sunlight gleams.
Sparkling wonders in frosty air,
A tapestry of white, so rare.

Children chase in joyous play,
Footprints mark the snow to stay.
In every drift, a memory made,
A tapestry of white displayed.

Soft whispers wrap the sleeping trees,
A gentle quilt, the softest breeze.
In stillness deep, the world is bright,
A tapestry of white, pure light.

As night descends, the stars arise,
Illuminating where beauty lies.
In moonlight's glow, we find delight,
Within this tapestry of white.

The Coldest Embrace

In shadows deep, the silence grows,
The coldest embrace that winter knows.
A breath held tight, under starry night,
Leaves the world in stillness, white.

Frosted winds weave through the trees,
Whispers shared on icy breeze.
Heartbeats echo, soft and slow,
In the coldest embrace, we flow.

Each moment lingers, crystal clear,
Time stands still when you are near.
In frozen hours, warmth holds tight,
The coldest embrace ignites the night.

A glance exchanged, as shadows play,
Love blooms bright in shades of gray.
In quiet corners, hearts set free,
In the coldest embrace, just you and me.

Through winter's grip, our spirits soar,
Finding warmth in what's in store.
Amidst the chill, our passions blaze,
In the coldest embrace, lost in a daze.

Frost-Kissed Whispers

In the quiet of the dawn,
Whispers of frost emerge,
Glistening petals shiver,
Nature's breath a gentle surge.

Underneath the silver sky,
Stars fade, the moon retreats,
Crisp air fills the waking world,
A dance of light in frozen streets.

Branches wear a crystal crown,
Each leaf trembles with delight,
Voices carried on the breeze,
Frost-kissed whispers take their flight.

Echoes of the night before,
Linger in the chilly air,
Silent secrets held in snow,
In this beauty, we stand aware.

Morning glows with softest touch,
Every breath a cloud of white,
Frosted worlds begin to play,
Magic brews in pure daylight.

The Chill of Dusk

As day surrenders to the night,
The chill of dusk descends,
Shadows stretch and merge with dreams,
Where daylight's whisper bends.

Soft hues fade to twilight grey,
Stars begin their gleaming show,
In the silence, secrets hide,
Beneath the veil of shadows' glow.

The wind carries a shivering tune,
Rustling leaves in cool embrace,
Nature pauses, holds its breath,
In this tranquil, sacred space.

Time slows down, the world stands still,
The chill deepens, calm and light,
Awakening the heart's desire,
For warmth and dreams to take flight.

And as the stars adorn the sky,
Each twinkle tells of distant lore,
The chill of dusk holds mysteries,
In shadows that forever soar.

Icy Fingertips on Silent Trees

Icy fingertips trace the bark,
As winter whispers soft and low,
Each branch draped in a frosty veil,
Ballet of crystals, pure in glow.

Silent trees in stoic grace,
Stand tall against the biting air,
Nature's canvas, white and still,
A quiet beauty, rare and fair.

In the twilight, shadows dance,
Beneath the weight of winter's hand,
Icy fingers weave their spell,
In forests deep, in winterland.

Each flake that falls adds to the peace,
A softening touch on every limb,
Nature rests in tranquil sleep,
While stars above begin to dim.

As night unfolds its chilly cloak,
The world beneath lies deep in dream,
Icy whispers roam the trees,
In silence, they weave their gleam.

Shadows Beneath the Snow

Beneath the blanket soft and white,
Shadows dance in layers of cold,
Silent stories, hidden truths,
In winter's grasp, they gently fold.

Whispers echo through the night,
A soft crunch underfoot, so near,
Each step reveals a tale untold,
In winter's realm where all is clear.

Branches bow with weight of white,
Crystals catch the moon's bright gaze,
In the quiet, nature breathes,
In shadows' play, the heart now sways.

Time moves slow, in rhythmic hush,
Embracing all that lies beneath,
In the cold, an ancient warmth,
Where shadows dwell in silent wreath.

As dawn approaches, soft and slow,
Melting dreams in morning's light,
Shadows shift, then disappear,
Beneath the snow, they take their flight.

A Dance of Snowflakes

In the hush of winter's night,
Snowflakes twirl in soft delight.
Each one whispers, pure and bright,
A ballet spun in silver light.

They scatter on the frosty ground,
A carpet white where dreams are found.
Together they drift, a silent sound,
In nature's arms, they twirl around.

The moon above casts a gentle glow,
Illumining the dance below.
With every flake, the cold winds blow,
A symphony of winter's show.

In this moment, time stands still,
As snowflakes dance, a timeless thrill.
Nature's art, with beauty filled,
A frozen joy, our hearts to fill.

So let them fall, these jewels bright,
In a world adorned in white.
Each flake a kiss, pure and light,
A dance of snow, a sweet goodnight.

Echoes of the Frozen Stream

Beneath the ice, the water breathes,
Echoes whisper through the leaves.
A melody of nature weaves,
In winter's grip, a song deceives.

The frozen surface glistens clear,
As shadows dance from far and near.
A haunting tune, both sweet and drear,
Calls to the heart, a longing sphere.

The wind carries tales of old,
Of streams that laughed and waters bold.
Now muffled voices, secrets told,
In icy depths, their stories fold.

Each crack and sigh, a frozen plea,
Reminds us of what used to be.
The stream awaits, a memory,
Of life that flowed wild and free.

As winter reigns, we pause and dream,
Of thawing days and sunlight's beam.
Yet in this cold, hear whispers gleam,
Echoes of the frozen stream.

Remnants of Autumn's Grasp

Leaves of gold and crimson bright,
Whirl in the crisp, fading light.
Nature's palette, a stunning sight,
As autumn whispers its gentle goodnight.

Beneath the trees, a carpet lies,
Nature's farewell in soft sighs.
Each rustling leaf, a soft reprise,
In the chill that soon will rise.

The air is thick with memories,
Of harvest moons and fading trees.
A dance of colors in the breeze,
As seasons change with graceful ease.

Yet in this loss, the beauty stays,
In vibrant hues of shorter days.
A lingering warmth that softly plays,
In the heart's embrace, autumn lays.

Though winter comes with its icy clasp,
We hold the warmth of autumn's grasp.
In every leaf, we feel and clasp,
The beauty of time, forever last.

Lanterns in the Cold

Beneath the stars, the night is deep,
While gentle frost begins to creep.
Like lanterns bright, our hopes we keep,
In darkest hours, our dreams we steep.

The chilly air, a breath of spark,
As flickers dance within the dark.
They light the way, a subtle mark,
Of warmth found in a world so stark.

Each lantern glows with tales untold,
Of whispered wishes and hearts bold.
In cold embrace, we gather gold,
A tapestry of dreams we hold.

Through winter's chill, we find our light,
In every soul, a flame ignites.
Together we shine, holding tight,
Lanterns in the cold, brave and bright.

So as we walk through frost and snow,
Let lanterns glow and spirits flow.
In every heart, love will bestow,
The warmth that only we can know.

Frost and Flame

In the morning light, frost gleams bright,
Whispers of warmth chase shadows away.
Crimson embers dance in the night,
The chill retreats, woven in play.

Ice and fire in a tender embrace,
A clash of worlds, both harsh and sweet.
In nature's heart, they find their place,
Binding all in a rhythmic beat.

Frozen lakes hold secrets untold,
Flames flicker softly, tales ignite.
In twilight's glow, stories unfold,
Frost and flame, a wondrous sight.

Glistening paths where starlight streams,
Heat from the hearth, a warm retreat.
Nature's harmony, woven dreams,
In every heartbeat, pulse of heat.

Together they dance, a fleeting sight,
As seasons turn, they coexist.
Frost and flame, a song of the night,
In their embrace, none can resist.

The Stillness Above

Stars hang like jewels in the deep,
A canvas of wonders, quiet and wide.
In the stillness, the cosmos sleeps,
Mysteries in silence, where dreams abide.

The moon whispers secrets to the night,
Casting shadows that gently entwine.
A dance of moments, pure and light,
In the calm, the heart learns to shine.

Clouds drift softly, a silver tide,
Carrying whispers from realms afar.
In this stillness, souls confide,
Finding solace in each shooting star.

The breeze sings low, a lover's tune,
Embracing the world, tender and true.
Night's blanket wraps the fading noon,
In the stillness, life begins anew.

Above, the heavens cradle our dreams,
Invisible threads of fate unite.
In the stillness, everything seems,
A symphony of peace and light.

Nightfall's Icy Breath

Whispers of dusk chill the warm day,
As shadows lengthen, the sky deepens.
Nightfall descends, a soft ballet,
In the silence, the earth still spins.

Frost-kissed air dances on my skin,
A shiver of magic in the air.
Moonbeams beckon, drawing me in,
Leading my heart to solace rare.

Stars awaken, twinkling bright,
Guiding the dreams that wander below.
Nightfall's breath brings gentle light,
A tender caress, a sweet glow.

In the quiet, thoughts begin to weave,
Stories of wonder, soft and deep.
With every sigh, the heart believes,
In the embrace of night, we steep.

So let the darkness wrap me tight,
Where fears dissolve, and hopes ignite.
In the calm of night's frigid might,
I find my way, the stars my flight.

Echoes of Solitude

In the silence, whispers dwell,
Echoes of thoughts that weave and twine.
Solitude's song casts a delicate spell,
In my heart, stillness feels divine.

Waves of memory crash like the sea,
Softly lapping against the shore.
In the quiet, I learn to be free,
In the absence, I long for more.

The trees sway gently, shadows play,
Each rustling leaf carries a sigh.
In the moment, I lose my way,
Yet find my truth beneath the sky.

A flicker of light in the endless dark,
Guides me through the spaces unfilled.
Echoes of solitude leave their mark,
In this hush, my spirit is thrilled.

Embracing the silence, I take a breath,
Finding solace where echoes blend.
In the heart of solitude, I rise from death,
For in this quiet, I learn to mend.

Cries of the Cold Moon

The moon hangs high in the frost,
Whispers echo, shadows lost.
Silver beams on winter's breath,
Cloaked in quiet, dreams of death.

Beneath its gaze, the world stands still,
Blanketed by the night's chill thrill.
Trees reach out with brittle hands,
Silent specters of forgotten lands.

In the distance, a howl does loom,
A call that stirs the cold, dark gloom.
Stars flicker like candles in the night,
Flickering phantoms, waning light.

Voices carried on the icy breeze,
Muffled sobs of ancient trees.
Cries of creatures hidden away,
In the embrace of shadows, they play.

The cold moon weeps in the still of night,
A sentinel lost in its silver light.
Its tears are diamonds on the ground,
In this expanse, a solace found.

Snow-Blanketed Stories

In the hush of falling snow,
Whispers of secrets start to flow.
Each flake dances, soft and light,
Weaving tales through the night.

Beneath the surface, memories hide,
Of laughter, love, sometimes pride.
Footprints vanish, lost in time,
Carried away, like a distant chime.

Branches bow with the weight of dreams,
Pillowed softly on silent beams.
A world transformed by icy grace,
Nature's canvas, a time and space.

Children's laughter fills the air,
Building forts without a care.
Snowmen stand with muffled glee,
Guardians of winter's mystery.

As daylight fades, the stars appear,
Illuminating stories we hold dear.
Each snowfall a page, a fleeting glance,
A snow-blanketed dance of chance.

Midnight's Frozen Symphony

At midnight's hour, silence sings,
Winter's breath on gossamer wings.
Notes of chill in the air collide,
With echoing dreams that never died.

Frozen trees like instruments stand,
Nature's orchestra, finely planned.
Crisp echoes of a world laid bare,
Harmony found in the frosty air.

Luminous stars play a gentle tune,
Light refracting from the cold moon.
As shadows swirl and gently sway,
In this symphony, night holds sway.

Snowflakes drift like silent keys,
A melody sung on a cold breeze.
Each flake falling with purpose clear,
Crafting a song only night can hear.

In the depths of the frozen night,
Music lingers, soft and bright.
Caught in a trance, the world in bloom,
Awaits the dawn, the end of gloom.

The Sheath of Silence

Wrapped in a cloak of white so deep,
Where the echoes of the world sleep.
A quilt of snow, soft and divine,
Hides the chaos, drawing a line.

Footsteps muffled, a ghostly tread,
In this realm where few dare to tread.
Whispers of winds lost in the fold,
Stories untold, both timid and bold.

The air is thick; nothing stirs,
Time pauses here, where silence blurs.
Nature breathes in a hushed embrace,
Waiting for dawn to unveil its face.

With each breath, the stillness hums,
In the distance, the echo comes.
Wrapped in peace, the heart finds grace,
A gentle refuge, a sacred space.

When the sun breaks, the silence fades,
Revealing the beauty the night parades.
Yet for now, in twilight's glint,
We cherish the silence, every hint.

The Last Leaves of Fall

The trees stand bare, their branches cold,
Whispers of summer in stories untold.
Leaves drift like memories, crisp and bright,
In the golden glow of fading light.

The ground is painted in hues of rust,
A canvas of autumn, a fleeting trust.
In the chill of dawn, they spiral down,
A farewell dance, a silent crown.

Every gust carries a secret sigh,
As they release their hold, goodbye.
In the crisp air, there's a bittersweet call,
Nature's farewell, the last leaves of fall.

Yet even in loss, there's beauty found,
In the quiet stillness that wraps around.
A promise of spring, beneath the frost,
In every farewell, it's never truly lost.

So let the wind play its gentle tune,
Through branches bare beneath the moon.
For every ending, a new start lies,
In the circle of life, where beauty never dies.

Celestial Tapestry in the Blue

Beneath the endless sky of deep cerulean,
Stars weave stories in patterns sudarian.
With each twinkle, a tale comes alive,
In the vast expanse, where dreams can thrive.

Clouds drift softly like whispers on air,
Carrying secrets we long to share.
The sun dips low, a brushstroke of gold,
In this tapestry where wonders unfold.

Moonlight dances on the tranquil sea,
Reflecting the dreams that long to be free.
Galaxies shimmer with vibrant delight,
Painting the canvas of the endless night.

Fireflies mimic the stars' gentle glow,
As night wraps us in a silken flow.
Each moment cherished under the light,
In this celestial weave, so pure, so bright.

Together we wander, hand in hand,
Lost in the beauty, a timeless land.
As we gaze up, our hearts intertwined,
In the celestial tapestry, love defined.

Gray Skies and the Promise of Thaw

Under the gray, the world feels still,
A blanket of silence, a winter chill.
Yet in the distance, a warmth starts to creep,
The promise of thaw within nature's deep.

Puddles reflect the clouds overhead,
Whispers of spring through branches spread.
As the frost melts, life stirs anew,
In the hush of the morning, life breaks through.

Crisp air carries the scent of the thaw,
A gentle reminder of nature's law.
Life cycles round, through dark into light,
In gray skies, dreams begin to ignite.

So let the clouds weep, let the rain fall,
For beneath the surface, there's beauty in all.
Winter's embrace may feel heavy and taut,
Yet spring's gentle touch brings warmth that can't be bought.

As days lengthen under softening skies,
Nature's revival, a symphony flies.
With hope in our hearts, we'll watch the earth grow,
Beyond the gray lies the promise of thaw.

The Silence of Twinkling Stars

In the calm of night, the stars softly gleam,
Silent watchers of our hopes and dreams.
Each twinkle a whisper, a secret shared,
In the vastness above, we feel love bared.

They dance on the canvas of deep, dark blue,
Each shine a reminder of all we pursue.
In stillness we ponder, our questions alight,
As the universe holds us, cradling tight.

Constellations echo the tales of old,
Guiding lost souls with their shimmer and gold.
A tapestry woven with wishes and prayers,
A silence that speaks of the burdens we bear.

The night deepens, the world drifts away,
In the quiet, we find a moment to stay.
With every gaze up, our spirits rise high,
In the silence of twinkling stars, we fly.

For in this embrace of the great unknown,
We discover ourselves, never alone.
In the vastness above, our worries dissolve,
In the silence of stars, we truly evolve.

Heartbeats Beneath the Ice

In winter's grasp, we hold so tight,
Our whispers dance through the cold night.
Beneath the frost, our hearts entwined,
In silent echoes, love defined.

Cracks in the ice, a subtle sound,
Each heartbeat felt, both lost and found.
The chill may bite, yet warmth we share,
A tender bond beyond compare.

As stars stare down from velvet skies,
We dream of fire, where hope will rise.
In every touch, the world stands still,
A perfect moment, hearts fulfilled.

With every breath, the night unfolds,
In chilly air, our story told.
We trace the paths of frozen streams,
While wrapped in love, we chase our dreams.

Through icy breath and snowy weaves,
Together here, our hearts believe.
No winter chill can tear apart,
The warmth alive within our heart.

Ethereal Landscape of White

A canvas pure, the world transformed,
In blankets thick, the earth adorned.
Each flake a whisper, soft and bright,
In frozen realms, a spark of light.

The mornings bloom with gentle grace,
As sunbeams kiss this tranquil space.
With every step, the silence sings,
In winter's touch, the joy it brings.

Trees draped in snow, a sculptor's art,
A peaceful hush that warms the heart.
Beneath the white, life waits in dreams,
In secret whispers, the spirit beams.

Footprints trace paths through soft embrace,
A journey born in this sacred place.
Where time stands still, the world fades slow,
In quiet awe, our spirits grow.

Golds and grays in evening light,
Bathed in shadows, the stars ignite.
In ethereal lands, our hearts take flight,
In this landscape of white, pure delight.

The Hush of Long Nights

In twilight's grip, a stillness falls,
As whispers hum through ancient halls.
The moon, a sentinel so bright,
Guides weary souls through deep of night.

Wrapped in blankets, warmth surrounds,
We listen close to the soft sounds.
Each heartbeat blends with night's refrain,
In quiet moments, peace we gain.

The stars peer down with gentle eyes,
Their silver light, a vast surprise.
In dreams we float on silken waves,
The hush of night, the heart behaves.

Outside, the world is draped in peace,
A pause that grants the mind release.
Beneath the weight of blankets, lost,
We linger long, we count the cost.

With every tick, the clock does play,
In its rhythm, we drift away.
In the hush of nights, our spirits soar,
To distant lands, forevermore.

Muffled Footsteps in Powdered Silence

In powder fine, the world feels new,
Each step we take is soft and true.
The air is crisp, a tranquil balm,
In winter's hush, the heart feels calm.

Muffled sounds in snowy haze,
We wander paths in winter's maze.
Footprints left, a fleeting trace,
In nature's arms, we feel the grace.

The pines stand tall, their branches bowed,
Encased in white, they're draped like clouds.
Our laughter dances in the air,
With frosty breath, we have no care.

Each moment captured, time suspended,
With every glance, our hearts befriended.
In this wonder, we lose our way,
In preserved stillness, here we stay.

As twilight falls, the sky ignites,
A canvas bold, with colors bright.
Muffled footsteps lead us home,
Through powdered silence, we will roam.

The Silent Season

In the hush of winter's grasp,
Nature holds her breath so still,
Blankets soft on cold ground clasp,
Time flows slow, yet bends to will.

Frosted trees like whispers stand,
Shadows dance in silver light,
Footprints trace in snowy land,
A world peaceful, calm, and bright.

Silent winds through branches weave,
Carrying tales of the night,
In this season, hearts believe,
In the magic of the white.

Stars above begin to glow,
Dreams lie cradled, safe and warm,
Through the silence, love will grow,
Wrapped in winter's gentle charm.

As the days begin to fade,
Every moment feels so rare,
In the silent season made,
We find solace everywhere.

Fields of Glimmering Silence

Fields stretch wide, a canvas bare,
Dew drops glimmer in the dawn,
Whispers linger in the air,
Nature speaks, though sound is gone.

Golden hues in sun's embrace,
Linger long on verdant blades,
In this vast, enchanting space,
Time stands still, the world invades.

Rustling leaves a soft refrain,
Nature's voice, a gentle sigh,
In these fields, we break the chain,
Of the hurried day's reply.

Among the blooms, our thoughts will wade,
Lost in echoes of the light,
Here in silence, dreams are made,
Underneath the starry night.

In the quiet, life unfolds,
Simple joys are buried deep,
Fields of silence, truth be told,
Guide us back to peace we keep.

Melodies of the Icebound Heart

Frozen streams in winter's grasp,
Echoes sing of love once bright,
Glistening in a crystal clasp,
The heart yearns for warmth and light.

Snowflakes dance through bitter air,
Every flake a whispered dream,
Melodies of loss laid bare,
In the silence, shadows gleam.

Through the frost, a flame remains,
Kindled deep within our soul,
Even in the coldest lanes,
Hope can rise to make us whole.

Icebound heart, still you shall beat,
Syncopated, soft and true,
In this chill, find what is sweet,
Love will guide you, start anew.

As the sun begins its climb,
Breaking free from winter's sigh,
Melodies of love in time,
Will unleash the warmest high.

The Breath of Morn's Chill

Morn awakens with a sigh,
Chill wraps round like a soft cloak,
Trees breathe in the amber sky,
Each breath whispers, words unspoke.

Frosty air, a painter's brush,
Colors bloom on nature's face,
In the stillness, blush and hush,
Every moment finds its place.

Birds begin their gentle calls,
Heaven's gate swings open wide,
In this space, the spirit stalls,
With the day as silent guide.

Across the hills, the shadows play,
Casting shapes on emerald ground,
In the chill of dawning day,
New beginnings, hope is found.

The breath of morn, a tender gift,
Holds the promise of what's near,
Time may whisper, hearts to lift,
In this chill, we find our cheer.

The Frozen Garden's Heart

In silence lies the sleeping ground,
A million whispers without sound.
Frosty petals, soft and white,
Guarding dreams within the night.

Beneath the ice, life waits in vain,
For spring to break this cold disdain.
With every breath, the chill remains,
Yet hope abounds, despite the chains.

Like crystal tears on every leaf,
The garden holds a quiet grief.
Yet even here, love's warmth will spark,
As shadows fade from deep and dark.

Patterns etched in frozen air,
Tell stories only few will dare.
To ponder on the beauty lost,
And find the treasures in the frost.

Hope will bloom, a vibrant start,
From the frozen garden's heart.
Awaking souls to dance anew,
In colors bright, in skies of blue.

Awaking from the Long Night

The stars have whispered tales of light,
As dawn approaches, soft and bright.
Frost gives way to warming sun,
Remembering the battles won.

All nature stirs from weary rest,
With each new breath, it feels refreshed.
A promise wrapped in morning's hue,
Awaking hearts in vibrant view.

The chill of night begins to part,
Unraveling the winter's art.
Buds begin to swell on trees,
As life returns upon the breeze.

With blossoms swaying in the light,
As earth rejoices from the night.
The world awakens, bright and clear,
With each new day, there is no fear.

The long night fades into the past,
Embracing warmth that comes at last.
In every shadow, glow and spark,
Awaking from the deep, cold dark.

Secrets Under the Snow

A blanket soft, of silver white,
Hides the whispers of the night.
Secrets slumber, deep and low,
Guarded well beneath the snow.

Each flake a tale, a memory's dream,
Of summer's laughter, a sunlight gleam.
Yet in this shroud, the past grows bold,
In silence kissed, the stories unfold.

Winter's hush, a gentle embrace,
Brought to life in a frozen space.
Nature's canvas, smooth and bright,
Holds the echoes of pure delight.

Underneath, the roots still churn,
Awaiting hints of spring's return.
In icy caves, the moments stay,
For life to emerge, come what may.

Secrets stir as seasons change,
In every corner, beautiful and strange.
Snow may cover, but cannot hide,
The hidden magic, deep inside.

Eyes of Winter

With piercing gaze, the cold winds blow,
Through frosty branches, quiet and low.
A world transformed, so stark and bright,
In the haunting eyes of winter's light.

The moon hangs low, a silver sphere,
Casting shadows that dance with fear.
But in the dark, there's beauty rare,
In the silent gaze of winter's stare.

The nights grow long, like whispered dreams,
Caught in starlight's softest beams.
Each moment held in breathless pause,
As nature rests without a cause.

Yet in the frost, a warmth still glows,
In icy realms where the wild rose.
Winter's eyes, sharp and clear,
Hold the echoes of life so dear.

So, let the cold winds weave their art,
For in the heart of winter's heart,
Lies beauty fierce with gentle grace,
In every frozen, sacred space.

Hushed Footfalls on Snow

Silent whispers through the night,
Softly treading, pure and white.
Each step a gentle, muted sound,
In this winter's peace, we're bound.

Underneath the silvered sky,
Footprints linger, yet we fly.
Chasing dreams in frosted air,
Magic dances everywhere.

Branches dressed in snowy lace,
Nature's art, a tranquil space.
Stars above begin to gleam,
This is life, a hushed dream.

Every flake a story tells,
Crystalline, where beauty dwells.
In the stillness, hearts unite,
Hushed footfalls in the night.

As dawn breaks with golden hue,
Snowy hills reflect the view.
A moment caught, serene and slow,
In the calm of freshly fallen snow.

A Canvas of Crystal

Shimmering under the pale moon,
Nature whispers a soft tune.
A canvas stretched beyond all sight,
Each facet catches stolen light.

Glistening like a thousand stars,
Covered trails and hidden bars.
With each glance, the world is new,
A treasure found in frozen blue.

Icicles hang like delicate art,
A masterpiece that warms the heart.
Fluttering shadows, pure and gold,
Stories of winter, quietly told.

Across the land, serene and bright,
Colors dance in soft twilight.
The breath of winter, crisp and clear,
In this canvas, love draws near.

Every corner, wrapped in white,
A dreamscape born of frosty night.
Nature sighs, and peace flows deep,
On a canvas that dreams to keep.

The Frosty Twilight

Twilight whispers, shadows grow,
A frosty breath begins to show.
Colors blend, like dreams at play,
As daylight slowly fades away.

The world adorned in silver glow,
In chilly air, a soft hello.
Stars awaken, twinkling bright,
In the hush of falling night.

Birch trees stand in graceful rows,
Wrapped in blankets, white as snow.
Each branch whispers ancient lore,
As time drifts gently to the shore.

While winter's beauty takes its hold,
A frosty tale begins to unfold.
Moments linger, tender and fleet,
In twilight's embrace, we feel complete.

Silence reigns, the world at peace,
In this time, all worries cease.
The frosty twilight, calm and still,
Wraps the earth in winter's chill.

Whispering Pines in the Cold

Whispering pines in winter's breath,
Holding secrets, embracing death.
Boughs are heavy, cloaked in white,
Guardians of the silent night.

In the forest, shadows creep,
Where ancient trees in stillness keep.
Frosted needles, a glistening sigh,
Beneath a dark and starry sky.

Echoes linger, soft and low,
Secrets shared where cold winds blow.
A gentle peace wraps every trail,
In nature's arms, we cannot fail.

As moonlight bathes the world in dreams,
The pines whisper soft, sweet themes.
Every sigh a tale retold,
Of warmth found in the bitter cold.

With every breeze, their song will rise,
In harmony with winter skies.
Whispering pines, eternally bold,
Carry warmth through frost and cold.

Frost-etched Memories

Whispers of the past remain,
In every silver seam of frost.
Echoes of laughter fill the air,
Time lost, but never truly tossed.

Beneath the chill, a warmth does hide,
In moments shared, in love's embrace.
Frost-etched memories glide,
A tapestry of time and grace.

Each flake that falls, a story spun,
Of joy and sorrow intertwined.
Under the pale and setting sun,
In every quiet sigh, we're confined.

Memories swirl like snowflakes dance,
Unique in form, yet all the same.
In winter's hush, we find our chance,
To cradle whispers, call their name.

Through glassy panes, we watch the light,
Transform the world in splendor bright.
In frost's embrace, we find delight,
In memories held, in shadowed night.

Twilight's Gentle Lament

The sky bleeds hues of crimson red,
As daylight softly turns to gray.
In twilight's grasp, our hearts are led,
To mourn the close of day's ballet.

With shadows long, the stars awake,
A tranquil hush blankets the land.
Each moment sighs, as dreams we make,
Slip through our fingers like warm sand.

Hope lingers here in the dusk's embrace,
A fleeting dance of light and dark.
We find our solace in this place,
Where silence leaves a tender mark.

The night descends, a velvet cloak,
Enfolding whispers of the past.
In twilight's arms, we softly choke,
On all the moments that won't last.

Yet in this sorrow, beauty gleams,
For every end births a new start.
In twilight's weep, we find our dreams,
And in our hearts, a pulsing art.

The Stillness of a Snowy Dawn

Morning breaks with gentle ease,
A quiet hush blankets the ground.
Each flake, a note in winter's breeze,
In stillness, hope and dreams are found.

The world adorned in white delight,
As daylight dances on the snow.
Nature's canvas, pure and bright,
Invites us all to take it slow.

Birds take flight, their songs ring clear,
In harmony with winter's chill.
A symphony for all to hear,
As time itself seems to stand still.

The air is crisp, each breath a frost,
In this serene and fleeting hour.
We ponder all that love has lost,
And find in stillness, hidden power.

As shadows stretch across the light,
The warmth within begins to rise.
In snowy dawn, our hearts take flight,
Awakening to silver skies.

Cold Hands, Warm Hearts

Fingers entwined, a breath of cold,
Yet warmth ignites beneath our touch.
In wintry winds, our love unfolds,
A sanctuary, it means so much.

The chill outside, a world of white,
But here, our hearts create a fire.
With laughter bright, we chase the night,
In every glance, desire.

We build our dreams like snowflakes tall,
Each tiny crystal, a work of art.
In this embrace, we have it all,
With cold hands, we warm our hearts.

A dance of shadows in the light,
As warmth flows from our grasping palms.
We face the storm, prepared to fight,
Finding courage in each other's charms.

So let the frost kiss our skin soft,
For in this world of icy rain,
Our love will twine, forever aloft,
Cold hands and warm hearts, their refrain.

The Weight of the Silent Air

In the hush of twilight's glow,
Where whispers of secrets flow,
Each breath feels thick as stone,
A quiet weight, we're not alone.

Shadows dance on the wall,
Silent echoes through the hall,
A canvas blank, emotions bare,
Painted with the weight of air.

The trees sway with gentle grace,
Bending low in this lonely space,
They seem to hold their breath as well,
In this quiet, we can dwell.

Stars above begin to fade,
In this silence, hearts cascade,
Yet in the stillness, truth we find,
An unspoken bond that binds.

As night wraps all in soft embrace,
We share this weight, this sacred place,
As time slips by without a care,
Together we breathe the silent air.

A Clockwork of Ice

Ticking softly, the gears align,
In a world where cold stars shine,
Each moment frozen in time's clasp,
Held together with a gentle grasp.

Crystals form on the window pane,
Reflecting dreams of warmth and pain,
Each tick a pulse of quiet grace,
A clockwork dance we cannot chase.

Bitter winds play a haunting tune,
Beneath the watchful silver moon,
The clock ticks on, relentless, slow,
Through the season's biting blow.

Hands of ice, they move with care,
Mapping spaces, tracing air,
Though frozen, life still finds a way,
In the heart of winter's sway.

With each turn, a story spins,
Of laughter, love, and weary sins,
In timeless grasp, we all must place,
Our dreams in this clockwork space.

Breathing through the White Veil

A breath is drawn in fresh, cold air,
Through misty shrouds that hide despair,
Each exhale forms a fleeting ghost,
Vanishing like the dreams we boast.

The world outside, a soft embrace,
Wrapped in white, a hushed space,
Footfalls muffled, a muted sound,
In this silence, solace found.

Wisps of frost curl in the breeze,
Carrying whispers from the trees,
They share their tales with quiet grace,
As snowflakes fall, a soft embrace.

Underneath the pastel sky,
We find ourselves, just you and I,
As time drips like melting snow,
In the veil, where dreams can grow.

With every breath, we come alive,
In this white world, we will thrive,
Through the veil, our spirits soar,
Among the quiet, we explore.

The Haunting of Frozen Footprints

Across the snow, the prints remain,
A story told of joy and pain,
Each step a memory etched in white,
Where shadows dance in soft twilight.

Crisp air carries a distant call,
Echoes of laughter, the rise and fall,
Of moments captured, frozen in time,
In the silence, a haunting rhyme.

Each footprint tells of paths once taken,
Journeys shared, hearts awakened,
In the still, the past resurfaces,
As the snow absorbs our verses.

Winter's breath on the landscape vast,
Holds the stories of the past,
Among the trees, their branches bare,
Whispers linger in the frosty air.

Yet with the thaw, the tales will fade,
But the echoes of love will cascade,
In the heart of those who dare,
To remember the footprints shared.

Nature's Frozen Melodies

In the stillness of the night,
Snowflakes whisper, soft and white.
Trees dressed in their icy gowns,
Nature's silence wears no frowns.

Streams beneath the frosty crust,
Murmur secrets, pure as trust.
Stars above twinkle so bright,
Guiding us with silver light.

Frozen lakes, a mirror's gaze,
Capture moments, time's sweet haze.
Footprints left, a story told,
In the chill, hearts grow bold.

The breath of winter fills the air,
Every sound dances, light and rare.
Nature holds her breath in peace,
In her grasp, all woes cease.

Underneath the moon's soft glow,
Nature's melodies ebb and flow.
In the quiet, magic lies,
Where the heart meets snowy skies.

Frosted Glass and Morning Light

Morning breaks, a golden hue,
Frosted glass, a world anew.
Each whisper of the dawn so clear,
Promises of warmth draw near.

The light spills through the icy panes,
Painting colors, soft refrains.
Nature wakes, a gentle sigh,
As shadows melt and dreams fly high.

Beams of sun on snowflakes dance,
Creating magic, sweet romance.
Frosted windows, art divine,
Glistening like a rare vintage wine.

Every droplet glows like glass,
Nature's artwork, time will pass.
In the stillness, beauty found,
In each sparkle, love unbound.

Morning light, a fresh rebirth,
Sharing warmth, spreading mirth.
Through the frost, hope takes its flight,
Kissing winter's cold with light.

A Dance of Icicles

Icicles hanging from the eaves,
Glistening like woven leaves.
In the breeze, they sway and gleam,
Nature's beauty, a frozen dream.

Each drip a note in winter's song,
Melodies sweet, where they belong.
A ballet on the edge of time,
Nature's rhythm, pure and sublime.

Reflecting sun, a crystal show,
Casting rainbows in the snow.
Frosted fingers reaching wide,
Nature's art, her icy pride.

Winds whisper soft, they gently sway,
Turning night to brightened day.
In their dance, a story told,
Of winter's heart, both fierce and bold.

Underneath the azure skies,
Icicles, like stars, do rise.
A frozen festival unfolds,
As winter's magic softly holds.

Sleet-Slick Streets

Sleet falls lightly, coats the ground,
   Whispers in the chilly sound.
   City lights shimmer and blur,
  As winter's breath begins to stir.

Reflections on these slickened paths,
   Echoes of winter's aftermath.
Step with care, the world transformed,
  In icy grips, new tales are formed.

Beneath the gray and cloudy skies,
   Life moves slowly, time defies.
   People wrapped in layers tight,
  Brave the cold with hearts alight.

Puddles form like mirrors still,
  Catch the light with a gentle thrill.
 A dance of raindrops on the street,
  Nature's pulse keeps steady beat.

As twilight falls, streets gleam bright,
   A wonderland awash in white.
  Sleet-slick streets, a canvas clear,
   Bringing winter's magic near.

The Last Breath of Autumn

Leaves whisper low, the end is near,
Golden hues fade, winter draws near.
The air turns crisp, a chill ignites,
Nature prepares for the longest nights.

Branches stripped bare, a somber sight,
Twilight lingers, day yields to night.
Pumpkin fields rest under grey skies,
As the last breath of autumn replies.

Clouds gather thick, a curtain of gray,
The sun bows out at the close of day.
With silent grace, the season unfolds,
A tale of warmth, in whispers retold.

Crisp apples linger, their sweetness stays,
In the heart of fall, in golden rays.
A fleeting moment, time drifts away,
The last breath of autumn will soon decay.

Icebound Dreams

In the stillness of night, a dream takes flight,
Frozen whispers dance in silvery light.
Beneath a blanket of crystalline sheen,
Icebound dreams shimmer, a magical scene.

Stars pierce the dark, twinkling so bright,
Reflecting the wonders, a breathtaking sight.
Each breath a vapor, a soft ghostly trace,
In this frosty realm, we find our place.

Winds echo low, like a lullaby sweet,
Guiding the heart with each gentle beat.
In the heart of the cold, warmth starts to gleam,
Lost in the wonder of icebound dreams.

Silent they stand, the trees made of glass,
Waiting for winter, letting hours pass.
Each branch a story, each flake a sigh,
Whispering secrets as the night drifts by.

Silent Snowfall

Snowflakes fall softly, a gentle embrace,
Covering the world in a white lace.
Footprints now hidden, the silence grows,
A hush envelops where no one goes.

The moon shines down on the blanket so pure,
As the quiet magic seems to allure.
Children awake to the glistening light,
With laughter and joy that shines ever bright.

Each flake unique, with patterns divine,
Falling like whispers, a soft, sacred sign.
In this moment, the chaos has ceased,
Silent snowfall, our hearts are released.

The world becomes wondrous, a canvas anew,
Painting our dreams in soft shades of blue.
In the still of the night, we find our way,
As silent snowfall gives birth to the day.

Shadows of the Frost

Morning creeps in with a frosty embrace,
Shadows are cast in this cold, silent space.
The breath of the earth, a mist in the air,
A tapestry woven with delicate care.

Crystals shimmer like diamonds in flight,
Reflecting the dawn, a magical sight.
Footsteps crunch softly on snow-covered ground,
With each passing moment, new wonders abound.

Trees wear their coats, all frosted and white,
Guardians standing through the long winter night.
In their embrace, dreams whisper and sway,
Carried by winds that lead us away.

Daylight reveals a world hushed and still,
Where nature's artistry reigns over all.
Shadows of frost dance with age-old grace,
In this peaceful realm, we find our place.